PEACEFUL PICKET NO.

COAL
CRISIS
DISCUSS
WAGES

NINE
DAYS IN
MAY

THE GENERAL STRIKE

Patrick Renshaw

NINE DAYS IN MAY

THE GENERAL STRIKE

Eyre Methuen London

For Donovan, Caradoc, Rhiannon and Richard

PICTUREFILE

First published 1975
by Eyre Methuen Ltd
11 New Fetter Lane, EC4P 4EE
© Patrick Renshaw 1975
Printed in Great Britain by
Butler & Tanner Ltd
Frome and London

ISBN 413 33260 8

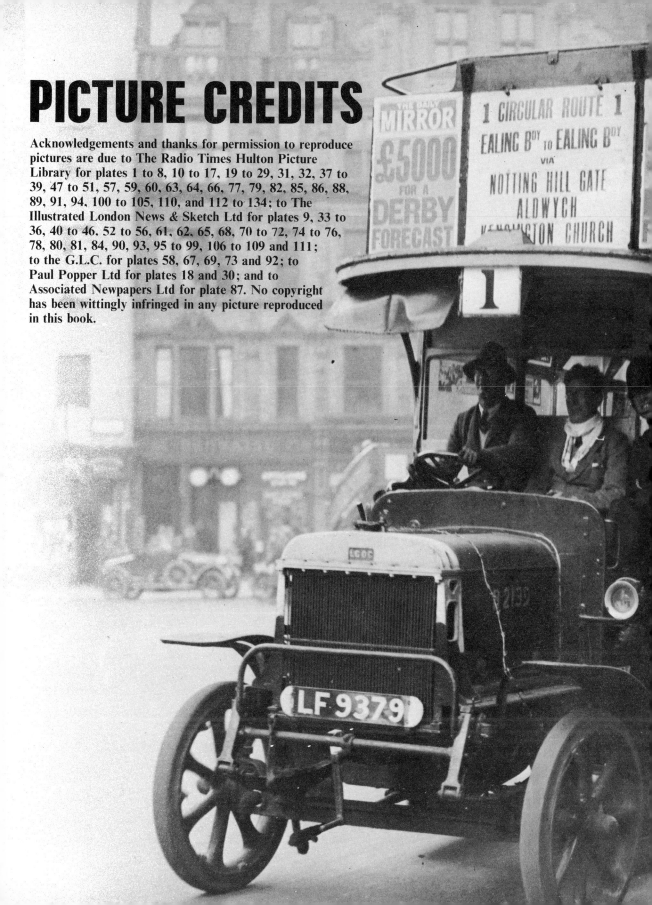

PICTURE CREDITS

Acknowledgements and thanks for permission to reproduce
pictures are due to The Radio Times Hulton Picture
Library for plates 1 to 8, 10 to 17, 19 to 29, 31, 32, 37 to
39, 47 to 51, 57, 59, 60, 63, 64, 66, 77, 79, 82, 85, 86, 88,
89, 91, 94, 100 to 105, 110, and 112 to 134; to The
Illustrated London News & Sketch Ltd for plates 9, 33 to
36, 40 to 46, 52 to 56, 61, 62, 65, 68, 70 to 72, 74 to 76,
78, 80, 81, 84, 90, 93, 95 to 99, 106 to 109 and 111;
to the G.L.C. for plates 58, 67, 69, 73 and 92; to
Paul Popper Ltd for plates 18 and 30; and to
Associated Newpapers Ltd for plate 87. No copyright
has been wittingly infringed in any picture reproduced
in this book.

INTRODUCTION

The folk memory of the General Strike is full of quaint period charm, redolent of the Gay Twenties. In the popular picture, undergraduates in Oxford bags drive buses and trains, medical students shift goods and luggage, and pretty typists thumb lifts to work in steam lorries and sports cars. All this happened, as the photographs in this book show. But it was only half the story. The other side was the desperation felt by millions of men during the Great Depression, when wages were low and unemployment high – and the camera also threw revealing light on the Two Nations which still existed in Britain in 1926. Those self-confident middle-class strikebreakers, with their pipes and plus-fours, those debutantes peeling potatoes perhaps for the first time in their lives, knew nothing of the lives of ordinary people. For though the strike brought industrial life to a standstill, it was not allowed to interfere with the social life of the privileged classes. Cricket continued, while audiences still flocked to opera, the theatre or night clubs.

With hindsight it is easy to minimise the danger of revolution. There were no deaths and only a few thousand arrests, while in Plymouth police actually played football with strikers. Certainly the mood of 1926 was less revolutionary than it had been in 1919. Yet the Prime Minister, Stanley Baldwin, believed Britain was closer to civil war than it had been for nearly three hundred years, while the novelist Arnold Bennett noted in his diary for 5 May 'General opinion that the fight will be short but violent. Bloodshed anticipated next week.' The tanks, armed convoys, troops in battle order, special constables and wrecked trains and trams pictured in these pages all testify that such fears were not entirely groundless. Ultimately, anxiety that if the strike continued it might get out of control persuaded the TUC to call it off when solidarity seemed unshakeable. The moderate leaders in London feared that real authority might soon pass to militants and revolutionaries in the regions. Rather than risk this they surrendered. The result was a legacy of bitterness, a sense of betrayal and a belief that if the strike had continued it would have led to victory.

This seems doubtful. The Government had all the aces and was determined to win. But no one can be sure what might have happened; and unfortunately, this is the kind of question which the camera cannot resolve. What it can do with greater clarity than words is dramatise the clash of the Two Nations and reveal the violence lurking just below the surface of events, as troops and pickets faced each other across the barricades of the class war. In the text of this book, and in the captions, I have tried to provide the framework. But the real story is told by the pictures themselves. For this I must thank the picture researcher, Thelma Schaverien, and the many anonymous photographers whose skill and courage made this book possible.

ORIGINS

The General Strike of May 1926, like Peterloo and Tolpuddle, has passed into the folk-lore of the nation. Its origins are familiar enough. It was called by the Trades Union Congress in support of the coal miners, who had refused to accept sweeping wage cuts and longer hours from the mine owners. But in a wider view its origins can be traced to the rise of socialism and organised labour in Britain. Indeed, the idea of a General Strike had first been advocated by William Benbow in the 1820s and 1830s. But Benbow's revolutionary ideas made little headway. Instead, after the failure of Chartism in the 1840s, British trade unions for the most part adopted moderate, cautious policies designed to improve the wages and conditions of skilled craft workers.

Victorian industrial growth and increasing prosperity favoured such an approach, and by the early years of the twentieth century organised labour had greatly strengthened. Trade unions had established the Trades Union Congress as a focus for its industrial activities, and the Labour Party to present its case in Parliament. Prospects looked good. Yet the decade before the First World War was a period of unparalleled labour unrest. With prices rising and real wages falling more sharply than at any time in living memory, employers tried to hit back at the more assertive trade unions, while the courts handed down legal decisions which injured them.

This increase in industrial disputes, strikes and class conflict was especially marked in coal mining. Coal had always been a hating trade. Mining was hard and dangerous, and though miners were better paid than many workers their living and working conditions were worse than most. They were tough and determined to press for more. The owners were obstinate, unsympathetic men anxious to cut costs to the bone in what was a highly competitive business. And since wages formed three-quarters of the cost of coal, wage disputes were endemic. In 1888, the miners had formed the Miners' Federation of Great Britain, and by 1914 the MFGB represented most of the million employed in the nation's largest industry.

More than one-tenth of the population was directly dependent on the miners, who dug a record 287 million tons of coal in 1913, of which more than one-third was exported. Coal was still the symbol of Britain's industrial greatness, and the miners were determined to share in this prosperity. Their struggle for a minimum wage in 1911–1913 excited the sympathy and even active support of other groups of workers, especially dockers and railwaymen. In April 1914, urged on by the miners, the railwaymen, dockers and transport workers' union joined to form the so-called triple industrial alliance.

The triple alliance was an informal organisation of some two million workers for sympathetic action during industrial disputes. However, on the outbreak of the First World War the triple alliance was put into mothballs as part of the industrial truce in face of the common enemy. The insatiable demands of the war economy guaranteed full employment and high wages. But prices rose even higher – and profits too. Though the mines, like the railways, were eventually taken under Government control as a war measure, the miners had protested bitterly against the level of profit being made by some owners, and there were strikes in South Wales and elsewhere. So inflation and profiteering helped revive pre-war industrial unrest and sharpen class conflict. Moreover, the war accelerated the process of social revolution and raised the level of expectation both at home and abroad.

The war destroyed the political and economic structure of Europe. Millions of men returning from the trenches in November 1918 found the world had changed out of all recognition. But they still sought assurance that their sacrifices had not been in vain. They wanted jobs, homes, security. At the same time, industrialists wished to continue the wartime boom, while financiers and bankers aimed at returning to pre-war stability and the gold standard. These aims in the long run were incompatible; meanwhile, in the euphoria of victory, the wartime boom was allowed to continue.

Economic prospects seemed promising in the mining industry. Yet the miners felt they were now less well paid relative to other groups of industrial workers. Moreover their union, the MFGB, having already achieved an 8-hour day, a minimum wage and then national wage agreements during Government control, was determined to secure full nationalisation of the industry as soon as possible. The mere suggestion that the Government might return the mines to the owners, who wished to cut pay and end national agreements, was enough to resurrect the pre-war solidarity of the triple alliance.

The unstable situation of 1919 was a bad time for Lloyd George to risk such a national stoppage. Rather than take on the triple alliance, Lloyd George's Government promised to retain control of mining and set up a Royal Commission to investigate the problems of the industry. The Commission, chaired by Sir John Sankey, represented miners, owners, industrialists and academics equally. Lloyd George promised to carry out its recommendations. But the very composition of the Sankey Commission, which seemed so fair, made divisions inevitable and so enabled Lloyd George to do virtually nothing. Indeed, its real significance was that it served to de-fuse a potentially revolutionary situation at a critical time. It enabled the Government to pass the point at which the general post-war discontent and labour militancy might have created a potentially revolutionary situation.

The next crisis came in 1920–21, when the post-war boom suddenly burst. Coal was perhaps hardest hit of all. Prices tumbled: losses amounted to £5 million a month between January and March, 1921. Anxious to divest himself of this responsibility, Lloyd George announced he would return the mines to the owners at the end of March. The owners posted sweeping pay cuts. Worse, they wished to scrap the existing system of national agreements and return to the hated old system of district rates.

But the miners' reluctant partners, such as Ernest Bevin, the dockers leader, and J. H. Thomas, of the railwaymen, were able to use unexpected divisions within the miners' own ranks to avoid action. Asked if he would abandon the 'pool' for the time being if he could secure a satisfactory wage settlement, Frank Hodges said the miners would be prepared to consider a settlement aside from the question of the pool. This answer was the crisis-point of the whole dispute. The Government offered to reopen negotiations immediately, and at an acrimonious and emotional meeting the following day the miners' executive decided by one vote to repudiate Hodges and reject the Government's offer. Bevin and Thomas said their unions could now no longer support the miners and called off the sympathetic strike.

The *Daily Herald* headline for the news summed up the mood: it read simply 'Black Friday'.

Black Friday was a disaster for organised labour and the miners. It marked the end of the triple alliance, or 'cripple alliance' as it was now bitterly called. The miners fought on alone for three months until they were forced back on terms worse than they might have had in April. Union membership fell with wages, while unemployment rose. But by 1925 prosperity had returned to many industries, especially those producing for the home market, while production was actually 10 per cent higher than in 1913. With the economy running smoothly, and the purchasing power of money slowly rising, unemployment remained at an apparently acceptable level of 10 per cent.

The stability of 1925 was in marked contrast to the unrest of the years just after the war. The politics of the transitional period were turbulent. In 1922 a Tory revolt overthrew Lloyd George's Coalition, and the following year a fatal illness forced the resignation of his successor, Bonar Law. His replacement was Stanley Baldwin, a Tory iron-master. But Baldwin's first steps seemed clumsy. In October 1923 he called a snap election and lost the comfortable overall majority he had inherited from Bonar Law. Liberal and Labour MPs combined to give Britain its first Labour Government under Ramsay MacDonald. To some it seemed like a dreadful portent of a socialist future. But dependent on Liberal votes in the Commons, MacDonald argued he was unable to pursue socialist policies and his Government lasted less than a year. In November 1924 Baldwin returned at the head of the largest Tory majority for half a century.

MacDonald was able to achieve a little for the miners. Since 1921 better times had returned to the coal trade. The miners' leadership had also become more militant. The pliable Frank Hodges, the miners' secretary, had been replaced by the demagogic A. J. Cook, from South Wales, while the laconic Yorkshireman Herbert Smith was now president of the MFGB. Cook and Smith took a democratic view of their job: the miners wanted no concessions so there must be none.

For the moment, the situation remained calm. With a Tory Government in complete command, the time seemed right for the return to pre-war parity the financial world had always deemed essential. Baldwin's surprise choice as Chancellor of the Exchequer, Winston Churchill, did not agree. But he was worn down by the insistent technical arguments of advisers like Montagu Norman and Sir Otto Niemeyer and finally took Britain back on the gold standard in April 1925. Grave damage was inflicted on sensitive export industries. By the early summer of 1925 coal exports were falling as steeply as they had in 1921. The industry was losing a million pounds a month, 400 pits had been forced to close, and probably half Britain's coal was being mined at a loss. The owners announced drastic new terms to meet the crisis. Wages would be cut to 1921 levels, the national minimum would go. With profits secure there was to be no limit on wage reductions – though if the miners would revert to the pre-Sankey situation and work an 8-hour day, the owners promised better terms. The MFGB refused to accept this ultimatum, and faced with the threat of a lock-out by the mine owners, turned to the TUC for help. The triple alliance was dead and buried. But the general council of the TUC had increased its authority and was able to offer a complete embargo on handling coal by its member unions in dockyards, in transport and on the railways. Unwilling to face such a confrontation at less than a month's notice,

Baldwin's Government reluctantly agreed to do what it had repeatedly said it would not do: pay the industry a subsidy in support of existing pay and profits for nine months. During this time another Royal Commission, this time under the respected Liberal Sir Herbert Samuel, would examine the industry. This was Red Friday.

The Samuel Report appeared in March 1926. It opposed nationalisation and the 8-hour day. It recommended national agreements, nationalisation of royalties, and sweeping reorganisation and improvements. But all this was in the future. Its only immediate proposal was a $13\frac{1}{2}$ per cent pay cut. The miners refused once more to look at this. A. J. Cook coined the irresistible slogan 'Not a penny off the pay, not a second on the day.' As Herbert Smith put it when Baldwin asked if he would make some concessions to persuade the mine owners to make some in their turn: 'Nowt doing. We've nowt to give.'

This intransigence reflected the problems of the mining industry. Baldwin's Government was also in an awkward spot. It did not like much of the Samuel Report. It did not want a national mining dispute or a sympathetic stoppage.

Negotiations dragged on through April. Then at the end of the month the MFGB and member unions of the TUC voted by an overwhelming margin to give full powers to the general council of the TUC to conduct negotiations with the Government, or call a General Strike, on behalf of the miners. Talks turned on whether the Government would continue the subsidy for a few weeks while plans to reorganise the industry were drafted. When reorganisation was started, the miners might then consider temporary pay cuts. Agreement seemed close. But on 1 May a million miners were locked out, and the TUC would bring out another $2\frac{1}{2}$ million workers on sympathetic strike on 3 May unless agreement was reached. The moderate leadership of the TUC, like Bevin and Thomas, was very reluctant to take this step. But when printing workers at the *Daily Mail* refused to set an article condemning the threatened General Strike, Baldwin used this as a pretext for breaking off negotiations. Within hours the General Strike had begun.

1. May Day in Hyde Park, London, on the eve of the First World War, with a Socialist Sunday School Union May Queen heading the procession

2. The human cost of coal, as bodies are brought up from Cadeby colliery disaster in July 1912

4. The Russian Revolution. Red Guards firing from an armoured car in
Moscow in November 1917

Miners protest against the wartime profits of the owners in August 1917

6. A mass meeting in support of the policemen's demands in Trafalgar Square, London

7. (*Far right*) A meeting at Tower Hill, London, learns of the collapse of the police strike

5. London policemen go on strike to secure union recognition in August 1919. They were joined by policemen in other cities, notably Liverpool

8. Pay day at the pit head. Miners' wages were cut by up to 50 per cent after the failure of the 1921 lock-out

David Lloyd George, the Coalition Prime Minister, who defeated the
rmans and the miners

10 and 11. Miners' pickets in the West Riding of Yorkshire advertise their demands during the 1921 dispute

12. Lloyd George with Sir Alfred Mond, one of the mine owners who had intelligent plans for dealing with the crisis in the coal industry

13. Miners from Mountain Ash
in South Wales

14. Mine owners arriving for
talks with the Government
during the 1921 mining dispute

Preparations to feed London during the threatened general stoppage in
21 with milk churns arriving in Hyde Park

16. Frank Hodges, secretary of the Miners' Federation of Great Britain, arrives for talks with the Government during the lock out of 1921

17. (*far left*) Thomas Marlowe, editor of the *Daily Mail*, who printed the forged Zinoviev letter which helped defeat the 1924 Labour Government

18. (*below far left*) Stanley Baldwin, the Conservative Prime Minister in 1925, with Montagu Norman, the Governor of the Bank of England, who persuaded his Government to go back on the Gold Standard in 1925.

19. Faced with further wage cuts in 1925 miners' leaders met the Government in talks aimed at averting a general stoppage in July

20. More miners' representatives meet the Government

21. Baldwin and Tom Jones, the deputy Cabinet secretary, arrive for talks with the miners. At the eleventh hour Baldwin agreed to pay a subsidy to the coal industry and set up a Royal Commission

22. Winston Churchill, Baldwin's Chancellor of the Exchequer, who had to find the money for the mining subsidy.

23 and 24. William Rust and Wal Hannington, two of the ten Communist Party leaders who were jailed in October 1925

5 (*right*) General Sir Herbert Lawrence, soldier, banker and industrialist, was one of the three other members of the Samuel Commission

6 (*below*) Sir Herbert Samuel, chairman of Baldwin's Royal Commission into the coal industry

THE NINE DAYS

The solidarity of the strikers surprised everyone, Government and TUC alike. Trade unions are not an army whose members obey orders without questions. Yet at a time of mass unemployment millions of men were risking their jobs, wages, benefits or pensions for which they had been paying all their working lives, to support the miners. The TUC had only called out the 'first-line' workers in transport, railways, printing, iron and steel, metal and chemical industries, building and power stations. Engineering, shipbuilding, textiles, woodworking, the Post Office and distributive trades were told to stay at work. But the effect of even this limited stoppage was dramatic. With more than $3\frac{1}{2}$ million workers out, the nation's industrial life came to a virtual halt. Mines, mills and factories closed. Public transport stopped. Most newspapers ceased production. The strange, oppressive silence of that first May morning seemed to many like the calm before the storm.

This response to the strike call was all the more remarkable since the TUC had made little or no preparation. The general council's moderate leadership was opposed to the idea of a General Strike. Moreover, it lacked the Government's resources, and feared that any effective preparations would be regarded as provocative. The Communist Party leadership had been jailed for incitement to mutiny in December, and the TUC was anxious to avoid a similar fate. Many leaders hoped that the Co-operative Wholesale Society, whose profit-sharing retail stores had grown with organised labour in the nineteenth century, would act, in Cook's words, as 'the victualling movement of the fighting forces of labour'. In fact, the organisation of the strike was a triumph of improvisation. Councils of Action appeared everywhere, running the strike at a local level, while at TUC headquarters in London Bevin and Walter Citrine, the new young general-secretary, took command of the central administrative machinery.

Preparations for the emergency on the Government side had been much more thorough. Since 1918, successive Government's had strengthened and streamlined plans that were first drawn up during the First World War. Top Civil Servants had divided the country up into administrative regions, each with their own means of maintaining essential supplies and services. This elaborate Government structure had been augmented since Red Friday by the appearance of an unofficial Organisation for the Maintenance of Supplies which recruited 100,000 volunteers to act as drivers, despatch riders, railwaymen, clerks and porters. Though dismissed by strikers as 'the plus-fours brigade' and 'people who had never worked in their lives' these volunteers, who immediately merged with Government personnel when the strike started, were instrumental in defeating it. Thirty years before a national stoppage on the railways would have been enough to halt the country. By 1926 the private motor car and the lorry enabled the Government to continue, thanks to the efforts of this volunteer army. Though some of these were recruited from the ranks of unemployed workers, the majority were ex-officers, medical students or Oxbridge undergraduates. Though the General Strike led to little bloodshed, and no deaths, it was still a class war.

Behind this army of volunteers, the Government had its real military and civil forces. Warships were sent to every major port in Britain, military convoys escorted food from the docks, tanks were stationed at Wellington Barracks, London, and guards at Royal residences were issued with battledress and 150 rounds of ammunition. A steel-helmeted Civil Constabulary Reserve was formed, and 200,000 special constables enrolled – 40,000 of them in London alone. Though the 4,000 arrests during the strike were a negligible proportion of the total number of strikers, more than 600 were made without warrant and there was much more violence than was generally realised. Even Plymouth, scene of the celebrated football match between police and strikers, saw ugly scenes, while there were riots at Edinburgh, Glasgow, Newcastle, Middlesbrough, Preston, Crewe, Nottingham, Swansea, and other industrial centres. Hull had a particularly serious riot, with 25 arrested and 41 injured, while London tram and bus depots saw constant clashes between strikers, blacklegs and police. The derailment of the *Flying Scotsman*, Britain's most celebrated express train, was a symbol of the dangerous passions the strike had aroused.

In addition, the Government had other powers. Banks were prohibited from transferring funds from European trade unions eager to support the strike, and some Cabinet members wished to stop strike pay, until King George V and others succeeded in persuading them that such a step would be dangerously provocative. More important, the Government dominated the news media during the strike. It published its own daily newspaper, the *British Gazette* which, despite the erratic editorship of Winston Churchill, managed to achieve a circulation of more than two million by the end of the strike. The *Gazette* denounced the strike as a threat to Constitutional Government, an argument which the TUC refuted in its own daily newspaper, the *British Worker*. Though better produced, and more restrained than the *Gazette*, the *Worker* was preaching mainly to the converted when it presented the strike as simply sympathetic action on behalf of the miners.

Moreover, the Government monopolised a much more potent means of communication in radio broadcasting. Some two million people had a licence to own the new crystal sets which became, in Beatrice Webb's words, 'The sensation of the General Strike'. Loudspeakers were set up in public places all over Britain, the British Broadcasting Company suspended its copyright so that local newspapers could republish its news, and five bulletins a day were broadcast enabling listeners to learn, in the revealing phrase of one of them, 'what was really happening'. The severe limitations on this knowledge were not properly known at the time. Churchill had wanted the Government to commandeer the BBC and run broadcasts direct. Baldwin and Davidson saw that it was much better to exercise indirect pressure. The young chairman of the BBC, John Reith, was anxious to support the Government and yet defend the integrity of organisation. The price of maintaining that independence turned out to be doing what the Government wanted. Thus news which might have encouraged the strikers was suppressed for the most part, while no representative of the TUC or the Labour Party was allowed to broadcast. An appeal for peace by the Archbishop of Canterbury was also suppressed, while the view of the Roman Catholic Cardinal Bourne that the strike represented 'a sin against the obedience which we owe God' was given the widest publicity.

Baldwin himself turned out to be a master of the new art of broadcasting. In a series of low-key fireside chats, which contrasted sharply with the hysterical tone of Churchill's *British Gazette*, he hammered home the

point that the strike was a threat to Constitutional liberty. If the TUC would call it off, and the miners return to work, he was a trustworthy leader who would ensure that justice was done. As the strike entered its second week there were unmistakable signs that this message was getting home to the people. The strikers remained as solid as ever. But the uncommitted people in the middle, many of whom had sympathised strongly with the plight of the miners at the beginning of May, were now starting to swing round behind the Government. Sir John Simon, a former Liberal Attorney-General, denounced the strike as illegal and said the strikers were liable to punitive damages, a view which was supported by Mr Justice Astbury in the High Court. Many respectable trade unionists were alarmed to discover that they might be breaking the law, and rumours were circulating that the Government meant to arrest the leaders, including the general council of the TUC. Further alarm was created by Churchill's sweeping announcement that any action undertaken by the armed forces in dealing with the strike would receive the Government's full backing. It looked like a prelude to a 'pogrom'.

At the same time, the TUC general council had been working hard to try to secure some kind of settlement. It exercised full power during the strike, and messages flowing into its headquarters in Eccleston Square showed spirits were high. But the moderate leadership, like Bevin, Citrine and Thomas, had never been very keen on the strike and feared success as much as failure. If extremists on the local Councils of Action in the regions seized control there was no telling what might happen. The TUC could find itself leading a real revolution, and bloodshed might ensue. Moreover, there were persistent organisational problems. The strikers had been allowed to issue permits so that essential goods and services could be delivered. But there was no clear definition of what exactly was essential, and many examples of non-essential goods getting through. Problems with the local Co-ops about their role during the strike were aggravated by demands from the 'second-line' workers that they be brought out too. So the general council's three key decisions during the strike were to refuse all money from Russia, to cancel all permits and call out the second line on 11 May.

Paradoxically, this last decision, which seemed to intensify the struggle, came less than 24 hours before the TUC's complete capitulation. When the strike was only two days old, Samuel had returned from Italy and begun unofficial negotiations with TUC leaders for a return to work. These talks lasted over the weekend and resulted in the drafting of the Samuel memorandum. This incorporated all the commission's points about wage cuts, reorganisation, a pay board and a basic minimum. There was therefore nothing surprising about it. The real weakness of the situation was that the miners had not been consulted and would not agree to anything which involved a reduction in wages. Indeed, Smith and Cook were unaware that any such negotiations were going on, and were very angry when they found out from newspaper reporters. By this stage, Smith was the really intransigent member of the MFGB executive. Cook could see the need for a national minimum wage, in his own phrase, 'not only with pluses above it, but minuses below it'.

But by the start of the second week of the strike, the TUC general council had clearly had enough and was simply looking for a speedy and honourable way out of their dilemma. They had never favoured the strike. They feared they might lose control in the regions to revolutionaries. Permits had created great bitterness, and relations with the Co-ops were bad. Moreover, there were real worries that, once the strike was settled, volunteer workers might retain their positions at the expense of the strikers. This fear was especially marked among railwaymen, who had the most to lose in terms of seniority, pension rights and so on, and thus constituted the weakest link in the TUC chain. Finally, it looked as if the general council were breaking the law, that they might be arrested, that strike pay might be stopped or Churchill launch violent counter-measures. In this mood the leadership's need to settle becomes easier to understand.

Yet even here, the TUC failed ignominiously. Despite repeated assurances given to Bevin and others, when the general council went to 10 Downing Street at noon on 12 May to call off the strike, Baldwin gave them no assurances about reinstatement or an orderly return to work, much less about getting the miners back. Bevin was incredulous. 'We have committed suicide,' he said. The strikers were equally unbelieving. Most hailed the first news that the strike had ended as a glorious victory for the TUC and the miners. What else could it be with everyone still so solid? Strike committees in Birmingham and elsewhere ran special 'Victory Bulletins', while even the *British Worker* carried a headline, 'General Council Satisfied That Miners Will Now Get A Fair Deal'. When they learned the truth they were stunned, just as Tory supporters were over-joyed to learn that the TUC's surrender really had been unconditional. Nevertheless, there were actually 100,000 more workers out the day after the TUC had officially called the strike off than there had been on 12 May, thanks to the strikers' sense of outrage and the reluctance of the second-line workers to go back so soon. But after that the collapse was sudden, the return disorderly, and victimisation, especially on the railways, widespread.

27 and 28. As the lock-out began on 1 May 1926 one million miners left pitheads all over the country

29. At the same time, tanks manned by steel-helmeted troops could be seen leaving Wellington Barracks in London

30. Workmen erected huts in Hyde Park, which was converted into a huge central food store for the whole of London

31. Milk was one of the most important foods stored in Hyde Park

32. Volunteer strike breakers queue in the forecourt of the Foreign Office in May

Volunteers at Work.

How London Carried on in the Strike.

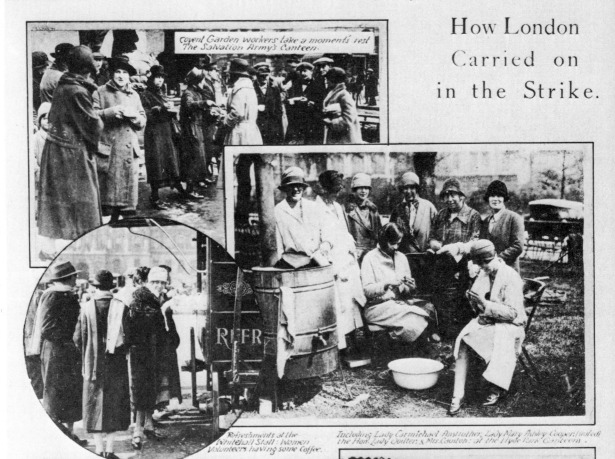

Covent Garden workers take a moment's rest: The Salvation Army's Canteen.

Refreshments at the Whitehall Stall: Women Volunteers having some Coffee.

Including Lady Carmichael-Anstruther, Lady Mary Ashley Cooper (seated), the Hon. Lady Coulter, & Mrs. Caxton: at the Hyde Park Canteens.

By the cook-house door in Hyde Park: Miss Morley, Lady Louis Mountbatten, the Hon. Mrs. Evelyn Fitzgerald, & Mrs. John Codrington.

Coffee for the lorry drivers in Hyde Park: Miss Morley, Lady Louis Mountbatten, Lady Forbes, Lady Gisborough, the Hon. Mrs. Evelyn Fitzgerald & Capt. Bundock.

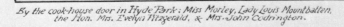

33 to 35. The privately-organised Organisation for the Maintenance of Supplies provided 100,000 volunteers, who merged with the Government organisation at the start of the strike

Kitchen Work in Hyde Park :

Society helps at Canteens.

ARMED WITH THEIR FRYING PANS : LADY BETTY BUTLER (LEFT) AND MISS COLLETT DOUGHTY.

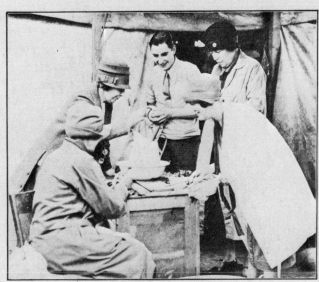

GETTING THE VEGETABLES READY : LADY LESLIE (TOP LEFT), MR. SIDNEY COXON, LADY ASKWITH, LADY LEIGH (BOTTOM LEFT) AND MRS. DENNISTOUN.

POTATO PEELERS AT WORK : MR. WILLCOX POLLEN, AND THE MISSES THORPE.

The Cook-house brigade at the Hyde Park Canteens for food supply transport men included many well known people. Lady Betty Butler is the younger daughter of the 7th Earl of Lanesborough and is the unmarried sister of the Duchess of Sutherland.

Lady Askwith is the wife of Lord Askwith, and Sir George Arthur Bt., M. V. O., was secretary to Field Marshal Earl Kitchener when he was Secretary of State for War.

INTENT ON HIS JOB : SIR GEORGE ARTHUR PEELING POTATOES.

THE VOLUNTEERS PLAY THEIR PART.

How all classes of the country came forward to perform national service.

UNDERGRADUATE VOLUNTEERS AWAITING TRANSPORT AT OXFORD
TO TAKE THEM TO THEIR TEMPORARY JOBS.

"SPECIALS" OFF DUTY WHILING AWAY
THEIR SPARE TIME AT A LONDON DRILL HALL.

MOUNTED "SPECIALS" OUTSIDE
BUCKINGHAM PALACE, SIR MICHAEL BRUCE
AND Mr. SAUNDERS.

BRITISH FASCISTI DISTRIBUTING
ANTI-STRIKE
PROPAGANDA IN THE WEST END.

VISCOUNT CURZON INSTRUCTING
A VOLUNTEER DESPATCH
RIDER AT THE HORSE GUARDS PARADE.

THE NEW CONSTABULARY RESERVE BEING INSTRUCTED
IN DEFENCE AND ATTACK.

THE "SPECIAL" REGULATES
STREET TRAFFIC.

UNDERGRADUATES OILING UP
AT KINGS CROSS PRIOR TO A RUN.

5. Volunteers unloading goods at one of London's main line railway
ations

37. Mucking out the stables at Paddington station was one of the tasks undertaken by this young woman volunteer. The young man behind her seems less enthusiastic

38. Lord Portarlington supervised the unloading of fish at Paddington station.

39. But though volunteers from the middle and upper classes won most
publicity, many of the strike-breakers were ordinary working men like these
lorry drivers playing between duty in Hyde Park

40. London streets were much more crowded than usual during the strike

Vol. CV N° 1373.   STRIKE EMERGENCY NUMBER   THE SPHERE MAY 15, 1926

The SPHERE

MAY 15, 1926.   Price : One Shilling.

Drawn by F. Matania.

41. London office workers travelling in improvised transport were
frequently helped by the police, as this drawing from *The Sphere* magazine
shows

42. Parts of the London
underground railway system
worked throughout the strike

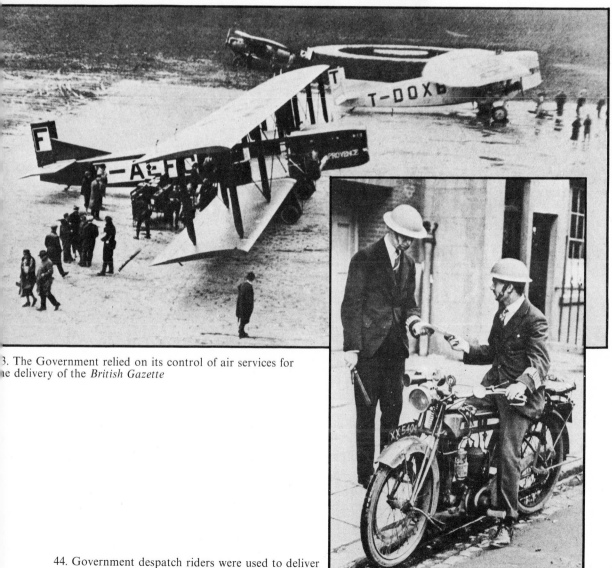

3. The Government relied on its control of air services for
he delivery of the *British Gazette*

44. Government despatch riders were used to deliver
messages all over the country

45. The TUC were not short of volunteer despatch riders

46. Despite the work of volunteer porters, goods traffic piled up at main line stations awaiting trains which never ran

47 to 51 The 'plus fours brigade' in action. Cheering
strike-breakers who had just passed their bus driving tests soon
found that the job presented unusual dangers. Guarded by
armed soldiers strike-breakers had to cover the engines of
buses with barbed wire to prevent strikers disabling the
vehicles. Drivers were usually accompanied by policemen or
soldiers for their protection

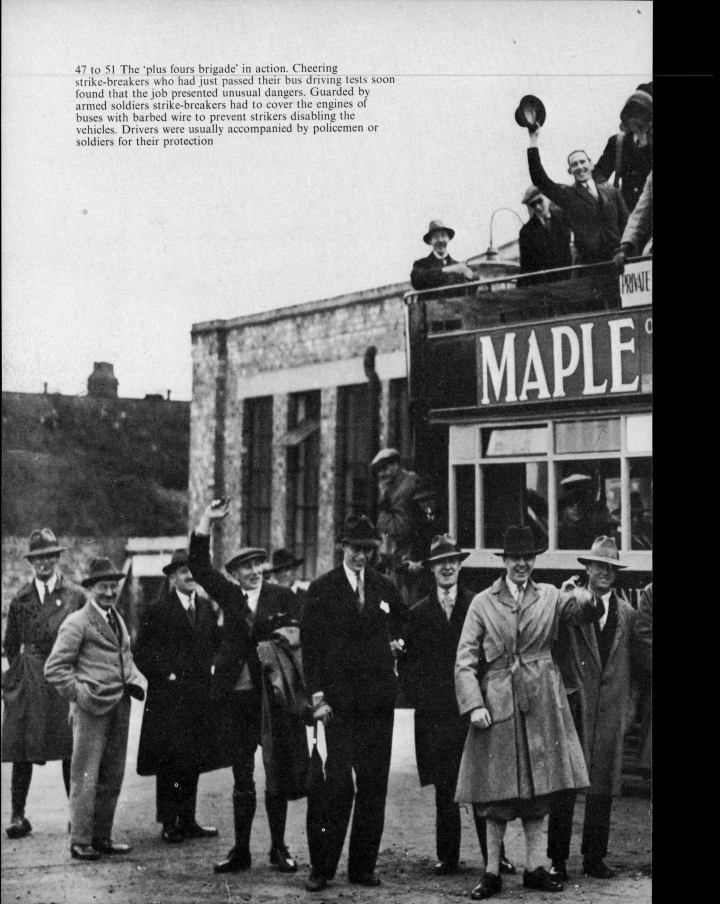

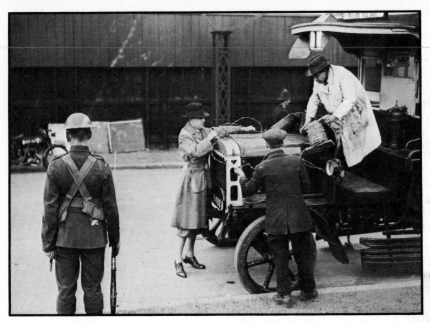

48

49

50

51

52. Despite the efforts of volunteer train drivers, like the Hon. C. R. Anson,
the railways were almost totally halted throughout the strike

53 to 55. Armoured cars were kept in readiness in London and elsewhere. Despite this, buses were frequently stoned and overturned by strikers, and passengers often had long waits for obliging motorists

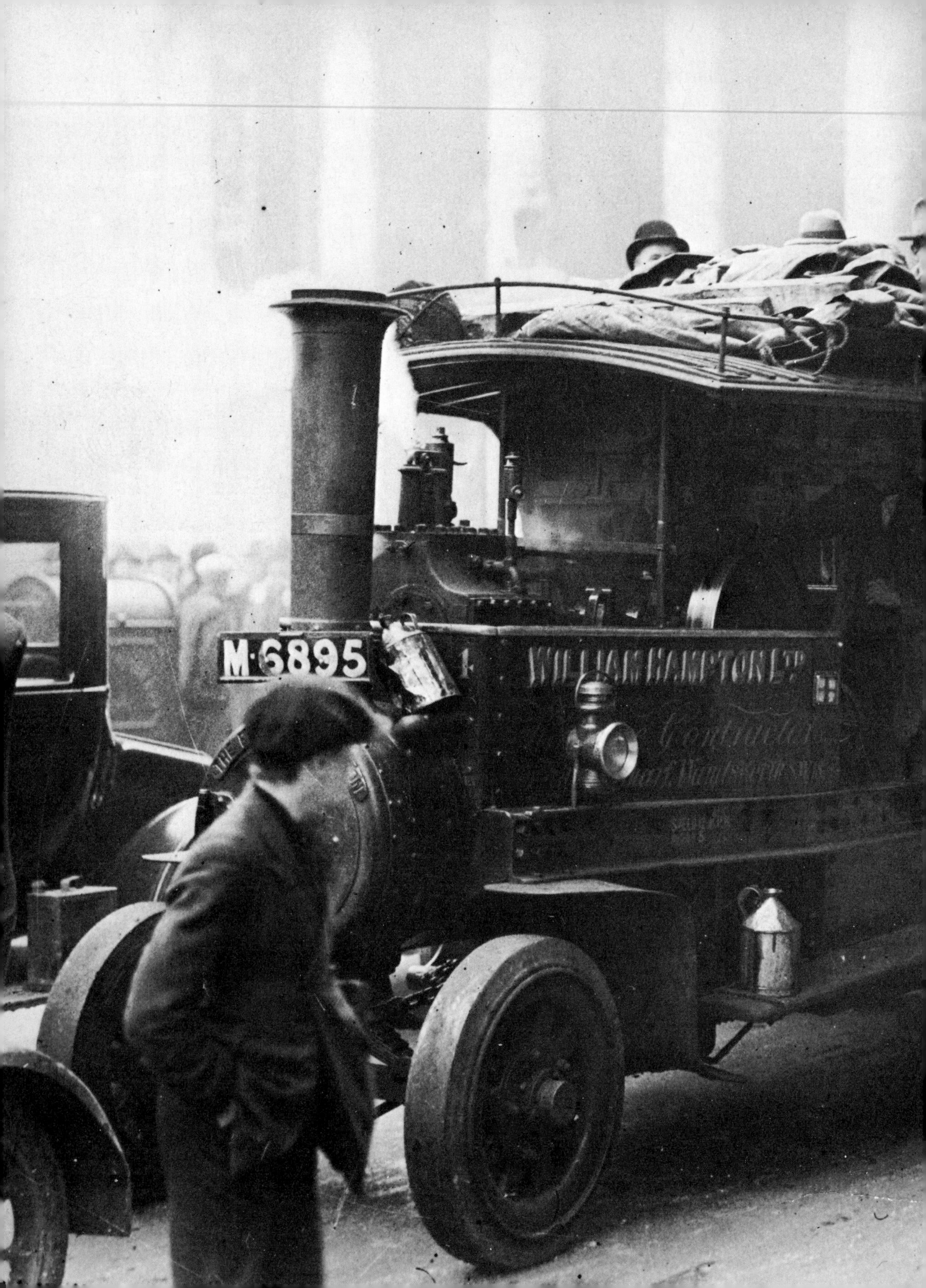
M·6895
WILLIAM HAMPTON LTD

56. A steam lorry and trailer packed with passengers passes the Stock Exchange

57. A disabled bus is towed through a crowd of strikers in Southwark, London

58. Police, strikers and users of private transport eye each other warily in Poplar in London's East End

59. Armed troops kept a constant
guard on buses at the transport
depots

60. Cavalry regiments, such as the
Royal Horse Guards, were ready for
action throughout the strike

61. Welsh guards with steel helmets
and rifles embark in charabancs at
Victoria Embankment for food
convoy duty

62 to 72. The military, rather than
volunteers, were used to maintain
essential food supplies

68

69

71

73. Pickets still managed to stop supplies being delivered on many occasions

CURIOUS EFFECTS OF THE STRIKE : UNUSUAL SCENES IN LONDON.

A MOTOR-BUS AS A RECRUITING OFFICE : VOLUNTEERS ENROLLING AT THE
L.G.O.C. EMERGENCY CAMP IN REGENT'S PARK.

AT THE TRADES UNION CONGRESS HEADQUARTERS AFTER THE STOPPAGE
OF THE STRIKE WAS ANNOUNCED : A CROWD OUTSIDE THE OFFICES.

A "TEST MATCH" IN ROTTEN ROW : VOLUNTEER WORKERS IN HYDE PARK
PLAY IMPROVISED CRICKET WITH STICKS FOR BATS AND BOXES AS WICKETS.

"A FLOCK OF SHEEP THAT LEISURELY PASS BY": AN UNUSUAL SIGHT
IN NEW BRIDGE STREET.

KEEPING UP THE DOMESTIC COAL SUPPLY IN THE EAST END OF LONDON :
PURCHASERS AT THE G.E.R. COAL DEPOT AT CUSTOMS HOUSE

ATTENDED BY WOMEN VOLUNTEERS AS WAITRESSES : VOLUNTEER WORKERS
ON THE UNDERGROUND RAILWAY AT A MEAL IN THEIR MESS-ROOM.

75. Loudspeakers were used to broadcast radio news bulletins

76 and 77. One of the most celebrated episodes of the strike – the football match between police and strikers in Plymouth. The Chief Constable's wife kicked off, and the strikers won 2-1

78. Sport continued as usual throughout the emergency, and the Australians carried on with their tour

79. The miners' executive leaving Russell Square for the fateful meeting with the TUC

80. Strikers in Plymouth attended a special daily service

81 and 82. The General Strike brought the Two Nations into conflict. Members of the more privileged classes often enjoyed strike-breaking. Others continued to go to the opera or night clubs

FIRST DAY OF GREAT STRIKE

Not So Complete as Hoped by its Promoters

PREMIER'S AUDIENCE OF THE KING

Miners and the General Council Meet at House of Commons

The great strike began yesterday. There are already signs, however, that it is by no means so complete as its promoters hoped. There were far more trains running than was the case on the first day of the railway strike in 1919.

The King received the Prime Minister in audience at Buckingham Palace yesterday morning.

Reports from all parts of the country indicate that satisfactory arrangements have been set up for recruiting. Volunteers came forward in large numbers in London and all the important provincial centres.

STRIKE LEADERS' MEETINGS.

The strike leaders have made no move, and the next step is with them.

The Executive of the Miners' Federation held a meeting yesterday morning at their headquarters. There was practically no business, and the officials then went to Eccleston-square, where the General Council of the Trades Union Congress were holding a meeting.

From Eccleston-square the whole Council, together with Mr. Herbert Smith, Mr. Cook, and Mr. Richardson (the miners' officials), went to the House of Commons. Mr. Ramsay MacDonald and Mr. Arthur Henderson had gone there half an hour earlier.

During the afternoon the full miners' Executive was sent out to the House of Commons to hold a conference with the General Council of the Trades Union Congress, and the miners and the Trade Union Congress special committee afterwards returned to Eccleston-square for a further meeting.

SPIRIT OF PUBLIC SERVICE.

Reports reaching the Government yesterday morning from the various areas into which the country is divided show that labour generally is quiet.

Recruiting stations have been opened in most parts of the country, and large numbers of volunteers have already enrolled.

RECRUITING STATIONS.

The following recruiting stations for volunteers in the London area are open:—

Hornsey Area: Faraday Urban District Council Offices, Euston U.D.C. Offices, Uxbridge U.D.C., and Harrow U.D.C.

Leyton District Area: Woodford U.D.C. Offices; Walthamstow U.D.C.; Ilford U.D.C., and Leyton U.D.C.

Hammersmith Area: Marylebone Town Hall, passing of U.D.C.; Kensington Town Hall; Staines U.D.C., and Westminster City Hall.

Bethnal Green Area: The Guildhall; Hackney Paper Library; Islington Old Town Hall; and Stoke Newington Public Library.

Wandsworth Area: Lambeth Town Hall, Wandsworth Town Hall; Richmond Town Hall.

Greenwich Area: Woolwich—32, Wilkinson-street, Westwerd; Deptford—Paradise and Union-road, Deptford.

Kingston Area: Kingston Town Hall; Wimbledon Town Hall; Epsom Rural District Council Offices.

Croydon Area: Catford Town Hall; Croydon Town Hall, Bromly Urban District Council Offices.

In the Home Counties stations have been opened at:—

Watford   Sittingbourne
St. Albans   Lewes
Colchester   Eastbourne
Chelmsford   Hastings
Hayes   Tunbridge Wells
Chatham   Brighton
Rochester   Guildford
Gravesend   Woking
Dartford   Reigate

NEVER-ENDING QUEUE.

The wooden huts in the courtyard of the Foreign Office were besieged yesterday by an eager crowd anxious "to do their bit." In the never-ending queue were representatives of every walk of life, fairly evenly divided between men and women.

Inside the huts the officials and their volunteer helpers had a hard time, with never a minute to look up from their work or to cease their strenuous fire of questions. "What can you do? What are you willing to do?" The answer to the first part of the question was usually something to do with motors, and the answer to the second question was invariably "anything."

FOOD SUPPLIES

No Hoarding: A Fair Share for Everybody

The Government is endeavouring to see that every person has a fair share of food and it is therefore of the greatest importance that every member of the public should assist in maintaining a fair distribution of supplies. They should do this by refraining from buying more than their usual quantities of foodstuffs.

Retailers should co-operate in securing a fair distribution of their stocks. Bakers generally are holding satisfactory stocks of flour and coal.

The Executive Committee, appointed by the London Division Exchange, unanimously agreed that all market prices established on Friday last for all kinds of butter, cheese, bacon, ham, and lard shall remain the maximum prices until further notice.

In some parts of the provinces there seems to be an inclination to put up prices, partly caused by a certain amount of panic buying, which, however, is being checked by the traders and Co-operative Societies themselves.

Milk services are being well maintained.

A MUSHROOM TOWN

The services of some of these volunteers were mustered in Hyde Park which, closed to the general public, controls the milk supply of London. In a night the familiar green stretches had changed into a mushroom town of ordered activity. Huts and tents had sprung up, each with an appropriate notice as to the occupation housed inside, and each in charge of competent staffs, who took to their unaccustomed duties with marvellous rapidity. One of the officials in charge of the milk post stated that the organisation was almost perfect. "When you consider the circumstances," he said, "something in the nature of a miracle has been achieved."

The commissariat arrangements for the vast number of men and women who pass through the park during the day and night are on the basis of the Y.M.C.A., who, in a huge marquee, never cease supplying hot drinks and hot food at the minimum price.

The milk lorries themselves form one continuous line from end to end and side to side of the Park. They bring the milk in from the farms, report to the transport officials, and receive instructions as to its distribution in London. Yesterday everybody seemed cheerful and hopeful, but quite prepared, if the worst came to the worst, to carry on their new activities indefinitely.

LONDONERS' TREK TO WORK.

On foot, squeezed into cars, standing in vans, riding pillion, pedalling on cycles, swarming Citywards by every road and route, London came yesterday morning doggedly and cheerfully to work.

Whoever has struggled along the choked highway to a-zoom zooms on every Day may form a mental picture of the first day's active pilgrimage to the East of Temple Bar. The congestion was so bad, and the temper of the people was so good.

No swaggerer came to many houses to tell whether the traffic had at the eleventh hour been averted, but to read the news on the not only to look out of the window. The articles with their press of private vehicles, with their streams of walkers setting to a long and steady stride, and will never a sign of not emotions of clamping trum, tole emphatically in print that the great general strike had begun.

Every thoroughfare was a one-way street—to London. The luxurious pace transitions and the drab and congesting relics of pre-war motoring crept along side by side in the crowded fraternity of the road. At every crossing the police beckoned on the unending line, and that task was made easy, because every man and woman at the wheel drove with consideration and a new courtesy.

In the inevitable blocks and jams, conversation rose above the throbbing of the engines. "How long will it last?" "They say that the Government—" And there was much of the forewarned chat that invariably is exchanged when two or three Englishmen are gathered together. "Was that Mr. Pott's first sample?" demanded a lorry driver stuck level, with a lorry machine whose equator oozed little rivulets. "Never mind," retorted the anxious owner. "I know, and"—indicating three laughing girls in the back seat—"I've a better cargo than you."

Every now and then there was something to cheer—a private 'bus carrying two and a half times its legal complement; a gallant driver adding yet another tired pedestrian to his overburdened car; a true party of blue-jackets marching out of Chelsea Barracks; an antiquated horse-brake with "Liver-nad-street" chalked on its crazy sides. With invincible good humour Londoners extracted satisfaction out of the very difficulties of their slow trek to town.

Many firms sent vans to bring in from the suburbs the most essential members of their staffs. Typists and girl clerks were briskly, confident of a lift, and waited everybody got to town, and the weary, and nevertheless

HOLD-UP OF THE NATION

Government and the Challenge

NO FLINCHING

The Constitution or a Soviet

When King and People understand each other past a doubt,
It takes a foe and more than a foe to knock that country out.

"Be strong and quit yourselves like men."
Kipling.

The general strike is in operation, expressing in no uncertain terms a direct challenge to ordered government. It would be futile to attempt to minimise the seriousness of such a challenge, constituting as it does an effort to force upon some 42,000,000 British citizens the will of less than 4,000,000 others engaged in the vital services of the country.

The strike is intended as a direct hold-up of the nation to ransom. It is for the nation to stand firm in its determination not to flinch. "This moment," as the Prime Minister pointed out in the House of Commons, "can been chosen to challenge the existing Constitution of the country and to substitute the reign of force for that which now exists.... I do not believe there has been anything like a thoroughgoing consultation with the rank and file before this despotic power was put into the hands of a small executive in London.... I do not think all the leaders who assented to order a general strike fully realised that they were threatening the basis of ordered government and coming nearer to proclaiming civil war than we have been for centuries past."

FEW LAMENT HEARTS

"There are few light hearts in England to-day," he reminded the House. "The only people who are happy in this situation are those who envy or who hate us, because they see the source of democratic freedom entering on a course which, it is possible at the time who enter on it, can only relieve time tyranny, and I have commerce in the contacts of our people, that we will see tame troubions through."

Mr. Baldwin ran rapidly re-echoed the statement made by the late Socialist minister of Labour (Mr. Tom Smart) only two years ago, who, when asked whether the Government would give full protection to men who refused to take part in illegitimate stoppages then in progress, said: "Yes, undoubtedly, the Government will do all in possible can to maintain public supplies." To that Mr. Baldwin added the assurance of the Government at the present crisis: "No man who remains at work and be prejudicially affected afterwards."

The Government, as the Chancellor of the Exchequer has pointed out, would gladly have made sacrifices provided care had been a reasonable prospect of securing agreement. Organised labour claims the right to strike as a means of getting a concession in trade disputes. "But that," he declared, "is an entirely different thing from the declaration, unstated, organised menace of a general strike in order to compel Parliament to do something which is otherwise would not do.

THE CHOICE

"The country and Parliament, which represents the nation, is confronted quite simply with the choice either of being ruled or of submitting to pay very large sums of the taxpayers' money to one particular trade which they do not think justified.... I cannot conceive any Parliament worthy of the name, for aims the true and strongest Parliament in the world, which would at any rate in a position which would submit to have its action dictated by such a menace.... This is a question, not of defeating the coal strike, but of defeating the attempt to coerce the whole community and to destroy the very foundations of our economic and political life. The Chancellor, however, foresees the nation's emergence from the struggle. "As one," he declared, "cat doubt what the end will be, but from every point of view, including our duty in the interests of the working classes of this country, we are bound to face this present challenge unflinchingly, rigorously, rigidly, and resolutely to the end."

He summed up the position as it now stands. "There is no question of there being a gulf across which no negotiator can pass. Anyone can approach the Government who has authority and can parley with them. The Trades Union Congress have only to cancel the general strike and withdraw the challenge they have issued, and we shall immediately begin with the utmost care and patience with them again the long, laborious task which has been pursued over these many weeks of endeavouring to rebuild on economic foundations the prosperity of the coal trade. No door is closed, but, while the situation remains what it is, we have no alternative whatever but to go forward unflinchingly as to our duty."

Meantime it is the nation to be strong, and quit it

COMMUNIST LEADER ARRESTED

Mr. Saklatvala, M.P., Charged at Bow Street

SEQUEL TO MAY DAY SPEECH

Mr. Shapurji Saklatvala, the Communist Member of Parliament for North Battersea, was arrested at his house, St. Alban's Villas, Riggegate, on Monday afternoon on a warrant charging him with inciting the police to commit a breach of the peace during a speech which he made on May Day in Hyde Park.

He appeared before Sir Chartres Biron at a special session of the Bow-street Police Court yesterday afternoon, and was remanded on bail until Thursday on the understanding that he would make no public speeches in the interval, except in the House of Commons.

Mr. George Lansbury, M.P., and Mr. Ben Spoor, M.P., drove up to the Court after the adjournment and each of them went surety for Mr. Saklatvala in £100. Mr. Saklatvala entered into a recognisance on his own behalf of £100.

Mr. Saklatvala was first arrested on Monday by chief Inspector Parker, of the criminal Investigation Department of Scotland Yard. He consented to say where he could be found when required, and was immediately released to go to the House of Commons. He was subsequently taken into custody at his house yesterday morning. Mrs. Saklatvala was present in the public gallery of the Court with a number of sympathisers.

Sir Travers Humphreys and Mr. E. Clayton appeared on behalf of the Director of Public Prosecutions, and Mr. W. H. Thompson appeared for Mr. Saklatvala.

Sir Travers Humphreys asked the Magistrate to take the same course in this case as was taken in the well-known case of Lansbury and Riley—that of requiring the defendant to enter into recognisances to keep the peace and to give such sureties as the Magistrate might think proper.

GOVERNMENT'S VIEW

"It is the view of the Government that their first duty is to keep law and order," continued Sir Travers. "Last Saturday in Hyde Park the defendant made a dangerous and inflammatory speech, which was most improper at the present time.... The defendant could have been charged under the Emergency Regulations, but it was decided not to adopt this course, since these are the first proceedings to be taken in the present state of affairs."

Detective-Sergeant Arthur Davies, who had taken a shorthand note of Mr. Saklatvala's speech, then gave evidence. Among the extracts from the speech read in Court were the following:

"The Union Jack has for generations done nothing but protect fools and rogues." "We want to tell the Army boys that they must revolt now and refuse to fight, and then they will be the real saviours of their homes and the workers. I want the Navy boys to march beside them."

At this point Sir Travers Humphreys remarked that the speech was one inciting the forces to abandon their duty.

Sir Chartres Biron—If it is very curious language if it was really used?"

Mr. Thompson then applied for a remand, stating that he had only just been instructed and had still to prepare the defence.

SPECIAL CONSTABLES

Appeal to Capable Citizens in London to Enrol

An appeal to capable citizens to join the Metropolitan Special Constabulary Reserve and assist the Metropolitan Police in the maintenance of law and order during the present emergency is issued by Mr. W. F. F. Horwood, the Commissioner of the Metropolitan Police.

The appeal is specially made to citizens not exceeding 45 years of age, to undertake these orders which are one of the most important bodies, to enrol and assume an uniformed upon those who set a value on law and loyalty to their King and Country and to the cause of good and ordered government.

Every effort will, he says, be made to minimise as far as possible interference with ordinary occupations. Those men enrolled will only be called on duty if and when the circumstances demand their services as requisite for the protection of the Metropolis. They will be released when the present crisis is over, though it they wish they may continue in the Special Constabulary Reserve.

Special constables who are injured in the execution of their duty, and widows and children in case of death, will be granted pensions allowances or gratuities.

It is desirable that a citizen should enrol at the enrolment station nearest to his own home.

Owners of motor-cars and motor cycles who are willing to attest as special constables and to drive their own vehicles should apply to the Commander, A.A. Section, 37-38, Long-acre, W.C. 2.

RESERVE OF OFFICERS

The Deputy Chief Civil Commissioner's Office issues the following:

The War Office states that there is no objection to officers of the Reserve of Officers offering their services to local organisations for the maintenance of order and vital services.

Those who do so will inform the local authorities of their potential military liability, which has priority over all other liabilities. Those whose services are accepted by local authorities will this prove be accepted and informed of when and where to and appointments.

THE "BRITISH GAZETTE" AND ITS OBJECTS

Reply to Strike Makers' Plan to Paralyse Public Opinion

REAL MEANING OF THE STRIKE

Conflict Between Trade Union Leaders and Parliament

A few words are needed to explain the appearance of the "British Gazette."

There are at present two quite different disputes which are holding up the country. The first is the stoppage in the coal industry. This is a trade dispute which could be settled in the ordinary way. The Government have already paid a subsidy of twenty-three millions to give time for this industry to put its affairs on a sound basis. They cannot, however, continue paying out between two and three millions a month of the taxpayers' money to the employers and workers in one particular trade.

Moreover, exporting coal at a loss to our rivals only increases their unfair competition with British manufactures. Lastly, if we go on subsidising our export coal Germany and other rivals will have to do the same. Thus every nation will be impoverishing itself in uneconomic competition. The coal industry must, therefore, come on to an economic basis.

The Coal Commission has shown how this can be done. The Government have accepted their proposals, and will carry out the recommendations affecting the State, even where this particular Government does not agree with them. But the owners and the miners must do their part as well. The owners have agreed to nearly everything recommended by its Commission; and it is certain that the small part to which they have not yet agreed would never be allowed to be sole block to the scientific reorganisation of the Coal Industry.

NO ADVANCE ON JULY.

The miners' leaders have not, however, made the slightest real advance towards an acceptance of those recommendations of the report which call for any sacrifice from them. In spite of the nine months' breathing space which has been obtained, or the twenty-three million pounds of public money which has been spent, or the fact that even with the subsidy there have been less than a hundred thousand miners unemployed in the coalfields, the leaders remain in exactly the same position as they were in last July. This may be natural, and one cannot help sympathising with the miners themselves in their difficulty. But it is no use making these difficulties worse by prolonging the subsidy or trying to carry on the coal trade month after month at a heavy loss.

All three parties—Government, owners, and miners—ought to accept universally the whole of the Recommendations of the Coal Commission. And if they do, and when they do, the Government, apart from doing its share, will not refuse a helping hand. So much for the trade dispute which has caused the stoppage of the coal industry.

On the top of this has now come a second dispute. The Trade Union leaders, having failed to induce the miners to make any concessions, have felt bound, nevertheless, to support them. They have, therefore, declared a General Strike and called out millions of men in carefully selected vital trades throughout the country. This has for the time being paralysed the whole business of the nation and prevented the crowded island from earning its daily bread by manufacture and commerce.

PROSPERITY AT STAKE

If the general strike is prolonged for many weeks the prosperity of Great Britain will be ruined for probably as many years. Our foreign rivals will eagerly supplant us in oversea markets. Unemployment, which had just slipped below the million, will rise again to an unprecedented heights. Uncertainty in insurance and all the working class funds will be exhausted, and hard times, such as were not known even during the worst of the war, will descend for a long period on the whole community.

The Trade Union leaders believe that this threat will compel the Government to grant the subsidy and prolong the subsidy the whole interests of the community as a

its interests, which ought to be paramount, but better than drinking salt water to relieve thirst. No one has posted this cut more strongly than the wiser and more responsible Labour leaders.

If Parliament were to allow its considered judgment to be overborne under the cruel assault of a general strike, the economic disaster would only be a part of a much greater disaster. It would definitely established that the will of a general strike which the Union leaders at present wield instable. These men, although it is tardily not the object of the great ny of them, would in fact become masters of the whole country, any power of government would passed from Parliament into hands. This would involve the of supersession of Parliament and representative institutions which have established in our land after hundred years of struggle, who have governed almost alone among nations of Europe, and which is foundation of our democratic freed.

NO SECTIONAL DICTATION

Instead of the representatives of our nation duly elected on a franchise almost universal, our rights and destinies would be in the hands of a body of men who, however well meaning most of them may be, represent only a section of the public and have derived no authority from the people comparable to that of the House of Commons. We must never forget, even in the heat and height of this struggle, that we are all fellow citizens. But for democratic State cannot possibly submit to sectional dictation. It is bound to defend and assert, no matter at what cost, the national and constitutional authority.

While, therefore, there is plenty of room for negotiation and a spirit of compromise about the coal trade, there can be absolutely none about a general strike. That is not a dispute between employers and workmen. It is a conflict between the Trade Union leaders and Parliament. And that conflict must only end, and can only end, in the decisive and unmistakable victory of Parliament. This victory his Majesty's Government is definitely resolved to secure.

Ample force to preserve the laws and the life of the nation is at the disposal of the State. But force is not the instrument on which a British Government should rely. We rely on reason, on public opinion, and on the will of the people. In this crisis the organisers of the general strike have made it their first care to paralyse public opinion by breaking down and muzzling the newspapers on which the whole people have been accustomed to rely for information about what is going on at home and abroad.

DANGER OF RUMOURS.

Nearly all the newspapers have been silenced by violent concerted action. And this great nation, on the whole the strongest community which civilisation can show, is for the moment reduced in this respect to the level of African natives dependent only on the rumours which are carried from place to place. In a few days, if this were allowed to continue, rumours would poison the air, raise panics and disorders, inflame fears and passions together, and carry us all to depths which no sane man of any party or class would care even to contemplate.

The Government have therefore decided not only to use broadcasting for spreading information, but to bring out a paper of their own on a sufficient scale to carry full and timely news throughout the country.

The British Gazette is run without profit on the authority and, if necessary, at the expense of the Government. It begins necessarily on a small scale, and its first issue cannot exceed 700,000 copies. It is proposed, however, to use the simulated resources of the State with the assistance of all loyal persons, to raise the circulation day after until it provides every man and woman in the country with full information and a guide all British citizens.

SPECIAL CONSTABLES

LAW COURTS AT WORK

Judge on the Duty of the Public

All the Judges in the Probate, Divorce, and Admiralty Divisions took their seats at the appointed time yesterday morning. Several King's Bench Judges were able to proceed with the trial of actions, but others had to delay proceedings because of late arrivals. Mr. Justice Barridge, in releasing a waiting jury, asked them to be, in attendance at a quarter-past ten on Wednesday morning. It is a public duty," he said, " and we must do the best we can."

When Mr. Justice Lawrence arrived late he said he had seen two motor-cars and a man coming. At-justice Hill stated that it had taken him two hours to travel from Wimbledon.

Mr. Justice Astbury said he did not propose to take any action in which the witnesses lived at any substantial distance. It would be a grave injustice to do so.

The spacious yard on the western side of the Law Courts resembled a huge garage, being packed with motors and motor-cycles.

G.P.O. SERVICES

Restrictions on Telegrams and Letters

The telephone and postal services are becoming so congested that delays will be inevitable unless messages and calls are considerably reduced.

Accordingly the public should avoid sending telegrams or making telephone calls unless of urgent matter.

No foreign or colonial parcels will be accepted and no letter or inland packet over the weight of eight ounces will be allowed.

There will not be a delivery of parcels in the London postal area.

THE KING RECEIVES THE PREMIER

The Prime Minister had an audience of the King at Buckingham Palace yesterday morning. He and his colleagues in the Cabinet were within call, and most of them attended the meetings of the two Houses, but no occasion arose for a Council nor for a meeting of the Negotiating Committee of the Cabinet.

Until the general strike is called off by the Trade Union Congress leaders nothing can happen. This is a condition precedent to any reopening of negotiations.

One result of the receipt of telegrams and telephone messages from the constituencies was that many members expressed the view that the Government ought to a p p l y accredited peaceful picketing. The proper numbers between men and men

MILK DISTRIBUTION

Control of Supplies in the Metropolis

The Deputy Chief Civil Commissioner's Office yesterday issued the following from the Board of Trade:

The Milk Distribution (Emergency) Order, 1926, dated 3rd May, 1926, made by the Board of Trade under Regulation 3 of the Emergency Regulations, 1926.

The Board of Trade, in exercise of the powers conferred upon them by Regulation 3 of the Emergency Regulations, 1926, and of all other powers them thereunto enabling, hereby make the following Order:—

(1) Every person owning or having power to sell or dispose of any milk within the Metropolitan Police Area of London shall as and when required by the London Milk Pool Committee, place such milk at that Committee's disposal.

(2) Infringements of this Order are summary offences under the Emergency Regulations, 1926.

(3) This Order may be cited as the Milk Distribution (Emergency) Order, 1926.

H. A. PAYNE,
A Secretary to the Board of Trade.

83 to 89. The Government
commandeered newsprint from *The
Times* to help produce its own
newspaper the *British Gazette* and
refused to allow John Reith, head of
the BBC, to let the Archbishop of
Canterbury broadcast

The Times

No. 44263   London Wednesday, May 5, 1926.   Price 2d

WEATHER FORECAST. Wind N.E.; fair to dull; risk of rain.

THE GENERAL STRIKE.

A wide response was made yesterday throughout the country to the call of those Unions which had been ordered by the T.U.C. to bring out their members. Railway workers stopped generally, though at Hull railway clerks are reported to have resumed duty, confining themselves to their ordinary work, and protested against the strike. Commercial road transport was only partially suspended. In London the tramways and L.G.O.C. services were stopped. The printing industry is practically at a standstill, but lithographers have not been withdrawn, and compositors in London have not received instructions to strike. Large numbers of building operatives, other than those working on housing, came out.

The situation in the engineering trades was confused; men in some districts stopped while in others they continued at work. There was no interference with new construction in the ship building yards, but in one or two districts some of the men engaged on repair work joined in the strike with the dockers.

Food – Supplies of milk and fish brought into Kings Cross, Euston and Paddington were successfully distributed from the Hyde Park Depot and stations. The Milk & Food Controller expects it will be possible to maintain a satisfactory supply of milk to hospitals, institutions, schools, hotels, restaurants and private consumers. Milk will be 8d. per gallon dearer wholesale and 2d. per quart retail today. Smithfield market has distributed 5,000 tons of meat since Monday.

Mails – Efforts will be made to forward by means of road transport the mails already shown as due to be dispatched shortly from London. The position is uncertain and the facilities may have to be limited to mails for America, India and Africa.

At Bow Street Mr. Saklatvala, M.P., who was requred as a result of his Hyde Park speech on Saturday to give sureties to abstain rrom making violent and inflammatory speeches, was remanded for two days on bail.

Full tram and (or) bus services were running yesteday at Bristol, Lincoln, Southampton, Aldershot, Bournmouth and Isle-of-Wight, and partial services in Edinburgh, Glasgow, Liverpool, Leeds, Northampton, Cardiff, Portsmouth, Dover, N. Derbyshire and Monmouthshire.

Evening papers appeared at Bristol, Southampton, several Lancashire towns and Edinburgh, and typescript issues at Manchester, Birmingham and Aberdeen.

The Atlantic Fleet did not sail on its summer cruise at Portsmouth yesterday. The men went on shore duty.

Road and Rail Transport – There was no railway passenger transport in Londor yesterday except a few suburban trains. Every available form of transport was used. A few independent omnibuses were running, but by the evening the railway companies, except the District and Tubes, had an improvised service.

Among the railway services to-day will be 6.30 a.m. Manchester to Marylebone; 6.30 a.m. Marylebone to Manchester; 10. 1C a.m. Marylebone to Newcastle; 9 a.m. Norwich to London; 9 a. m. King's Cross to York; 3 p.m. King's Cross to Peterborough; 9 p.m. Peterborough to King's Cross. L.M.S. Electric trains will maintain a 40 minutes service. On all sections of the Metropolitan Railway except Moorgate to Finsbury Park, a good service will run to-day from 6.40 a.m.

The Underground hope to work a six minutes service on the Central London Line today from 8 a.m. to 8 p.m. between Wodd Lane and Liverpool Street. The following stations only will be open:- Shepherds Bush, Lancaster Gate, Oxford Circus, Tottenham Court Road, Bank, Liverpool Street. A flat fare of 3d will be charged.

The Prime Minister had an audience of the King yesteday morning.

There was no indication last night of any attempt to resume negotiations between the Prime Minister and the T.U.C.

The Government is printing an official newspaper, "The British Gazette" which will appear today, price 1d. It will be distributed throughout the London area.

Volunteers for the London Underground Railways and for L. G. O. C., omnibuses should communicate with the Commercial Manager's Department. 55 Broadway, S.W.

The Prince of Wales returned to London from Biarritz last night, travelling from Paris by air.

LATEST London BULLETIN

No. 10   REGISTERED

Thursday, May 6th, 1926.

STRIKE
LATEST NEWS

THE STATE of affairs throughout the country is about the same.

THE PRIME MINISTER sates that no person that remains at work shall be prejudicially affected afterwards.

10,000 WORKERS that were called out at Billingham (Durham) reported for duty, ignoring Strike notices.

FOOD. It is authoritively stated that the supplies of food and fuel are sufficient to maintain the country for many weeks.

All L.C.C, Schools are being kept open.

OWING TO STRIKE difficulties, the sollowing London Theatres have decided to close:—Apollo, Shaftesbury, His Majesty's, Winter Garden, St. Martin's, Adelphi, Gaiety, Savoy

WIRELESS NEWS will be broadcasted by the B.B.C. (circumstances permitting), at the following times—10 a.m., 1 p.m., 4.0 p.m., 7.0 p.m., 9.30 p.m., 10 p.m., 11 p.m., 11.45 p.m.

FORTY TRAMCARS are running at Plymouth.

ATLANTIC FLEET. Insted of the whole Atlantic Fleet leaving for a summer cruise, only Submarines and Destroyers sailed.

MANY VOLUNTERS Enrolled at Hyde Park as Lorry Drivers.

SMITHFIELD. Only one cold storage works was open yesterday.

BILLINGSGATE. 400 tons of fish arrived yesterday morning.

HOW TO GET HOME. Met announce the following trains.
Uxbridge to Baker Street hourly from 8.20 a.m.
Harrow to Baker Street ½ hourly from 6.40 to 8.10 then every 15 minutes.
South Kensington to Liverpool Street every 15 min, from 7.55 a.m.
Aldgate to South Kensington every 15 min. from 8.5. a.m.
Hammersmith to Paddington and vice versa every 15 min.

STOP PRESS
NO CHANGE

It was announced that the Government would not resume negotiations until the General Strike Notices were withdrawn.

There will be no racing at Chester to-day.

TEA. The Tea Buyers Association have formed a committee so that tea will be distributed evenly.

HOSPITALS. The London Hospital has closed the outpatient department owing to strike difficulties until further notice,

BANK RATE. No change.

TAXIS We are informed that the taxi-drivers have joined the Strike, but there are still a number on the roads.

UNDERGROUND All underground lines in London will be open to-day.

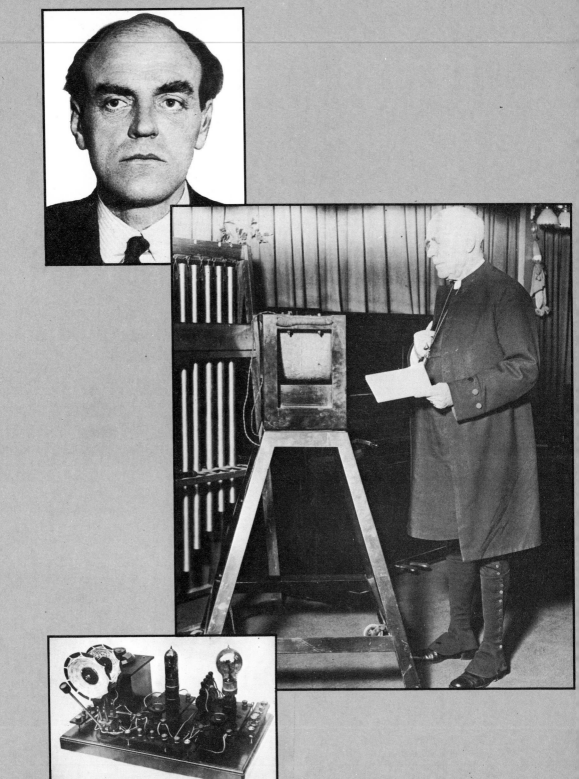

90 and 91. Sir Herbert Samuel
returned to England from Italy
to conduct unofficial negotiations
with the TUC. On arrival at
Dover Major Henry Segrave, the
racing driver, drove him to
London

92. Strikers in London's dockland were
demoralised by the success of the
Government's army food convoys

93. Demonstrations continued throughout the strike

94. Mounted police preparing to make a baton charge on demonstrators at the Elephant and Castle, London, where a bus was pushed down a subway

95. The Flying Scotsman express, en route from Kings Cross to Edinburgh,
was derailed by strikers near Newcastle on 11 May. No one was hurt, but
the incident caused widespread outrage. Four people were killed in five rail
crashes caused during the strike by inexperienced volunteers

a. Special constables guarding a barricade at the entrance the meat market at Smithfield

b. Strikers at Plymouth arriving at St. Andrew's church for a special daily service during the strike

Pickets intercept a L.M.S. railway clerk working outside general office at Crewe

d. How the nation was kept informed: reading the wireless bulletins at Marconi House, Strand

97. 1 Ernest Bevin, one of the most influential members of the TUC general council
2 A. G. Walkden, general secretary of the Railway Clerks Association
3 Robert Shirkie, of the Colliery Engineers, Alonzo Swales, the most left-wing member of the TUC general council, and A. J. Cook, the miners' secretary
7 Leaders of the Labour Party played a passive role during a strike. Here Ramsay MacDonald (*centre*), the Leader of the Opposition, and Arthur Henderson, his deputy as Leader of the Labour Party, go on a walkabout with J. H. Thomas, a former Labour Cabinet Minister, leader of the railwaymen and a member of the TUC general council
8 A. J. Cook, the militant socialist, in an uncharacteristic bowler hat
9 Herbert Smith, 'the man in the cap', the laconic president of the Miners' Federation of Great Britain, leaving a meeting

98. 1   Sir William Mitchell-Thompson, who as Chief Civil Commissioner was in charge of the Government machine for defeating the strike
2   His Principal Assistant Commissioner, A. B. Lowry
3   Major W. Cope
4   Major Sir Philip Sassoon
6   Capt. H. Douglas King
9   Major G. Hennessy
10   Lt. Col. G. F. Stanley

11   Capt. D. H. Hacking
13   Major Earl Winterton
These were the men who controlled the apparatus for dealing with the emergency
14   Sir William-Joynson-Hicks, Home Secretary
5   Coal-owners representatives
8   Minister of Labour: Sir Arthur Steel Maitland
12   Parliamentary Secretary to the Dept. of Mines: Col. G. R. Lane-Fox

99. The Prime Minister relaxing at Chequers with his family

100. (*Left to right*) Lord Birkenhead, Neville Chamberlain and W. E. Guinness arriving for a Sunday Cabinet meeting during the strike

101. (*Left to right*) Sir William Mitchell-Thompson, the Chief Civil Commissioner, goes to a Cabinet meeting with Joynson-Hicks, Sir Philip-Cunliffe-Lister, President of the Board of Trade, and Sir Samuel Hoare, who was in charge of distributing the Government newspaper the *British Gazette*

102. Two key figures on the TUC side, Arthur Pugh (*left*), chairman of the TUC and Walter Citrine, the secretary

103. The beginning of the end – Ramsay MacDonald, Arthur Henderson and Ben Tillett leave TUC headquarters in Eccleston Square to seek terms

104. The Prime Minister slips out of 10 Downing Street with his PPS, Sir Ronald Waterhouse

105. (*Left to right*) J. H. Thomas, the most conciliatory member of the TUC general council, leaving 10 Downing Street after talks with W. C. Bridgeman and Sir Ernest Gowers, of the Mines Department

106. Arthur Pugh, leaving 10 Downing Street after calling off the strike. Walter Citrine looks pleased

107. John Bromley, of the railway footplatemen, was anxious to end the strike because he feared his own men might start drifting back to work

108. Ernest Bevin leaves 10 Downing Street after the surrender in angry mood. Despite repeated assurances, the TUC negotiating team had made no attempt to secure any conditions

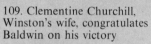

109. Clementine Churchill, Winston's wife, congratulates Baldwin on his victory

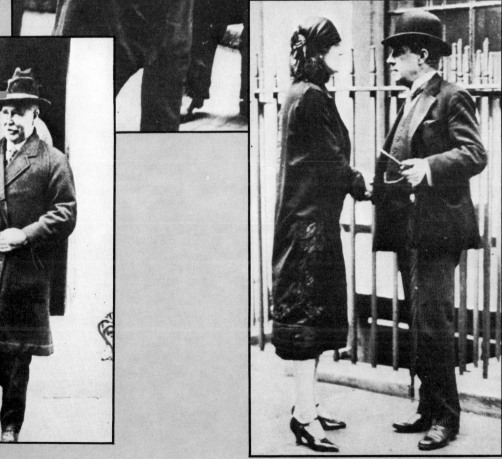

110. Some of the 200,000 special constables autograph their batons before being disbanded

111. But the miners' lock-out continued for another seven months. Here Herbert Smith and W. P. Richardson leave a national conference of miners

112. By September some miners were drifting back. Here Smith and Richardson continue their discussion after leaving an MFGB conference in London

113. A. J. Cook talks to reporters as it became clear that the miners would have to go back on whatever terms they could get

114. MFGB delegates face defeat at the November Conference in Kingsway Hall

115. Miners at Biltow, Staffordshire, had returned to work by August 1926

AFTERMATH

Deserted once more, as they had been in 1921, the miners fought on alone, this time for seven months. Of the Cabinet, only Churchill seemed interested in trying to put some pressure on the owners to settle on terms which would have done something to save the face of the MFGB. The owners, for their part, were determined to use the situation not only to force wages down, but to smash the miners' union once and for all. In this they had some success, for by the end of the strike tens of thousands of miners began drifting back to work and some of them, especially in the more prosperous regions such as Nottinghamshire, joined the new 'Spencer Union', founded by George Spencer, a Labour MP from Nottingham, along lines of collaboration and company unionism. Helped by their own efforts, money from other unions and from overseas, especially Russia, and most important from Poor Law relief administered by Boards of Guardians, the miners were able to survive. But by November 1926 they had been forced back by hunger on the worst possible terms. District settlements replaced national ones, the eight-hour day was imposed by law, and wages were back to the low point of 1921 and in some places to 1914 levels. The capitulation of the TUC in May had been a prelude to catastrophe for the miners.

The Tory Government lost no time in securing the fruits of victory. The 1927 Trade Disputes Act made the General Strike illegal, and punished the Labour Party by hitting the financial link between them and the unions. The miners had been helped by the Poor Law Guardians, and now the Minister of Health, Neville Chamberlain, who during the General Strike had said 'the best and kindest thing to do now is strike quickly and hard', disbanded those Guardians he felt had been too generous in relieving hunger and suffering. Meanwhile, the Two Nations, having come into conflict in May 1926, proceeded on their separate ways. Unemployment remained steady at 10 per cent of the insured population, but was much higher in certain trades and regions. Among miners alone it ran at around 400,000 as hundreds of pits were forced to close, while in the depths of the Great Depression, in 1929–31, the total jobless figure rose to nearly three million. Yet for those lucky enough to enjoy regular work the picture was far less bleak. The purchasing power of money continued to rise, and while the Jarrow Crusade and the other Hunger Marches of the 1930s dramatised the protest against mass unemployment, suburban semis could be bought for around £500, and the middle class enjoyed the benefits of the private car.

It took the British labour movement 20 years to recover from the failure of the General Strike. The Labour Party landslide at the polls in 1945, and the full employment which followed the war, enabled trade unions to heal much of the hurt and humiliation which the failure of 1926 had symbolised. Yet at the same time the defeat shocked the TUC into a new world. The General Strike was thirty years out of date when it occurred. After 1926 there could be no return to direct action and the politics of class conflict. The Mond-Turner talks in 1928 on cooperation and partnership between both sides of industry may not have yielded many results at the time. But they influenced TUC thinking, especially the thinking of such leaders as Ernest Bevin, for years to come.

At first sight the General Strike appears to confirm that politics were based on class conflict. The Two Nations, of unemployed members and underfed children on the one hand, and the Gay Young Things of Evelyn Waugh's *Diaries* on the other, certainly clashed during the strike. So did miners and owners, TUC and Government. But the divisions within their ranks were equally important and revealing of much greater complexity. Finance and industry were also at loggerheads. Indeed, the strike was really precipitated by the decision to go back on the gold standard, which confirmed the subordination of industry to finance. Churchill took the decision, but the pressure for it had come from the Treasury and the Bank of England. Churchill came to regard it as the worst decision of his life. It led to high unemployment and low wages, but also stable prices and rising real incomes. To make this policy work, the Government had first to take on the TUC and force down the miners' wages. For this reason, the General Strike was not only the most dramatic, but also the most decisive, event in British domestic politics between the wars.

116. Another reminder of the human cost of coal with the explosion in 1927 at the Marine Colliery, Cwm, near Ebbw Vale. These anxious women await news of their men.

117. Crowds wait for news of the 40 men still entombed at Cwm. At that stage 14 bodies had been brought to the surface. The final death toll was more than fifty

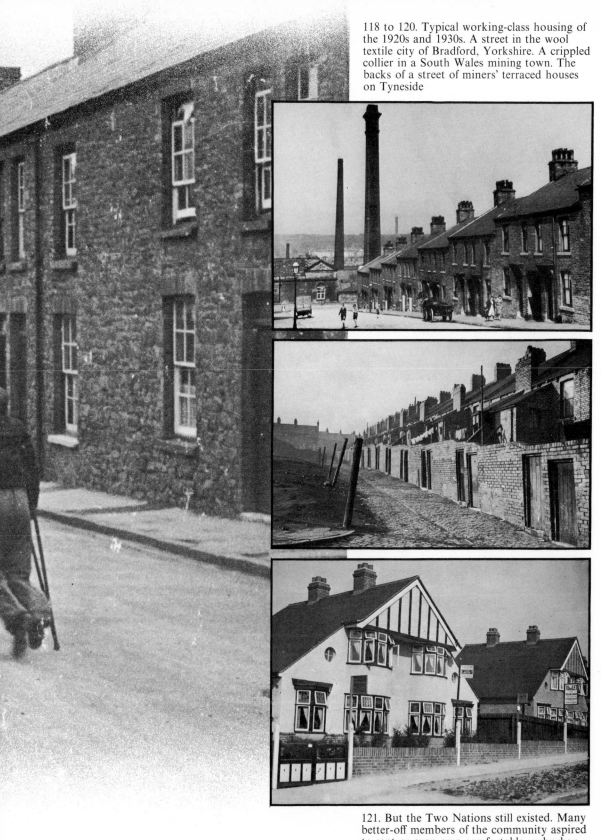

118 to 120. Typical working-class housing of the 1920s and 1930s. A street in the wool textile city of Bradford, Yorkshire. A crippled collier in a South Wales mining town. The backs of a street of miners' terraced houses on Tyneside

121. But the Two Nations still existed. Many better-off members of the community aspired to rent or even own comfortable surburban semi-detached houses like these, or run a small family car

122. Guests at a Charity Ball at Grosvenor House were unaware of the real plight of the nation's poor

123. Miners at pit bottom in a Durham colliery wait for a safety check

124. Unemployed miners scratching for coal on a Tyneside slag heap were able to sell it for a few shillings to be spent on food

125 to 133. The Hunger Marches of the 1930s were what really brought home the extent of poverty. The unemployed marched from as far as Scotland to try to bring pressure to bear on the Government. Pipe and drum bands helped to keep spirits high, and the marchers ate corned beef, potatoes and beans on the journey. In London mounted police cleared marchers from the Edgware Road in October 1932. The most famous Hunger March was the Jarrow Crusade of 1936. Jarrow, a shipbuilding town in the industrial North-East with one of the highest rates of unemployment in Britain, was known by its inhabitants as 'the town that was murdered'. But it is doubtful if any of the Hunger Marches achieved very much. Middle class opinion was radicalised, as it was by the rise of Fascism and Nazism in Europe and the mounting threat of war. But nothing effective was done to alleviate mass unemployment. Deflation led to a steady rise in the purchasing power of money and most people felt the benefit of this

129

130

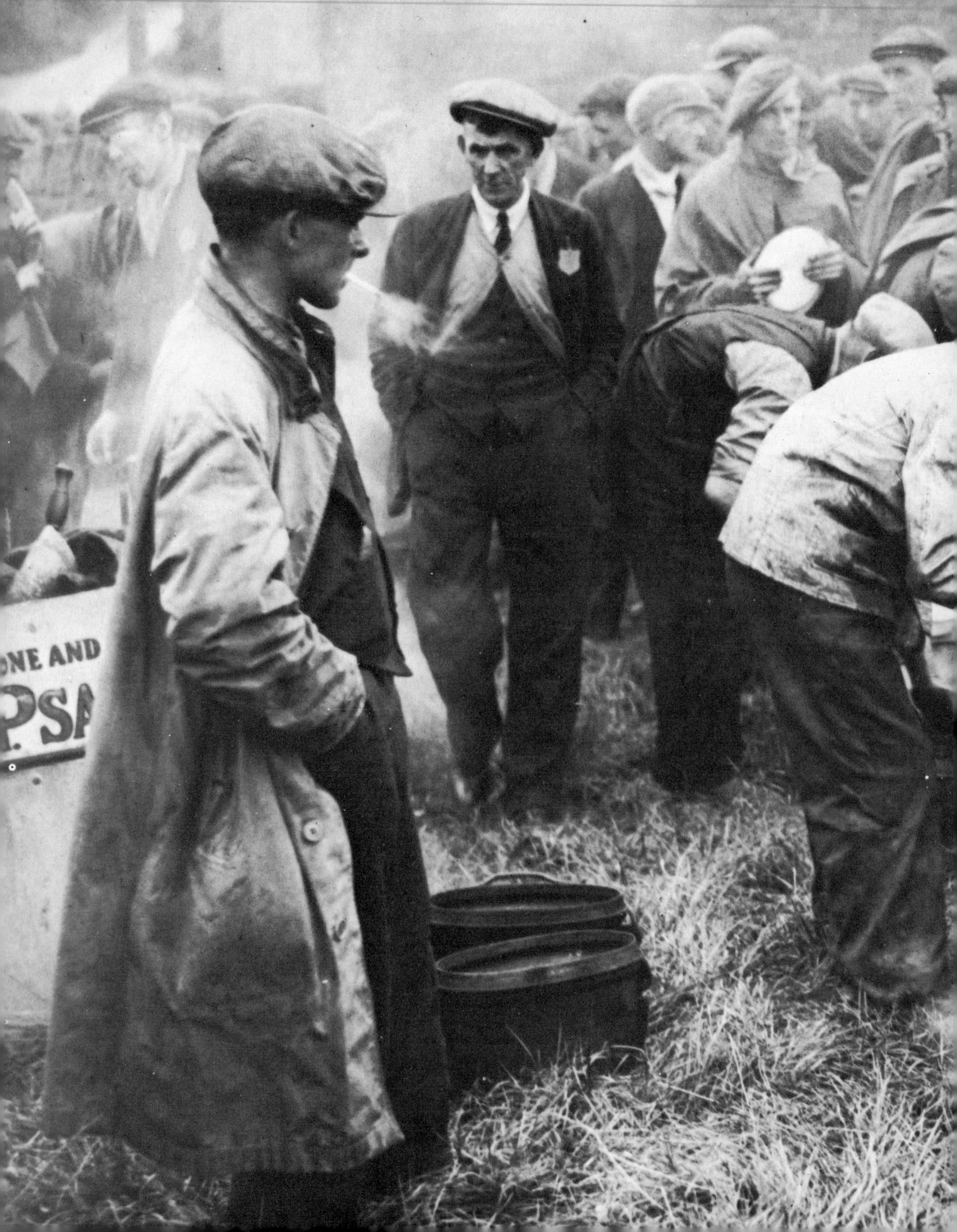
ONE AND
PSA

134. A street scene in Wigan in the 1930s. Ten out of
15 mills, 17 out of 40 pits were closed in what had
once been a thriving industrial community. Nearly
10,000 men were jobless in a total population of
85,000. George Orwell entitled his famous book about
the Great Depression *The Road to Wigan Pier*